MOST
SECRET

Published by IWM, Lambeth Road, London SE1 6HZ
iwm.org.uk

First created by M.I.9 in 1942

First published in 2023 in this format

ISBN 978-1-912423-67-5

A catalogue record for this book is available from
the British Library.

Printed and bound by Gomer Press Limited

Colour reproduction by DL Imaging

Every effort has been made to contact all copyright holders.
The publishers will be glad to make good in future editions
any error or omissions brought to their attention.

www.carbonbalancedprint.com
CBP2275

MOST SECRET

•

M. I. 9 ESCAPE

AND

EVASION DEVICES

•

CONTENTS

PART ONE

INTRODUCTION

We grappled with what to call this splendid volume. It has official titles — *M.I.9 Technical* and *Per Ardua Libertas* — but neither of these hint at what is within if you are unfamiliar with the war work of this secret department. It lives in the rare books section of IWM's library, and we wanted to reveal its contents to a wider audience, as it deserves to be much better known. We have chosen *Most Secret* as the title, which appears at the front of the original volume; it was also the highest British security classification at that time, indicating the importance and confidential nature of what it contains. We hope you enjoy this introduction to the early years of M.I.9 — an ingenious branch of Second World War military intelligence, tasked with assisting evaders and escapers.

The book contains illustrated descriptions of various escape gadgets created by M.I.9 such as silk maps, compasses and ration boxes among other items, and indicates how these were smuggled into prisoner(s) of war (POW)

camps. It is almost an exact reproduction of the original M.I.9 volume, except for the cover, this introduction and the accompanying source list. It has also been reduced in size to fit a more conventional format. Printed by the Sun Engraving Company Limited and bound in red Moroccan leather with gold tooling, the album was produced in very small quantities. Sun Engraving were one of the largest printing companies in Britain and produced other intelligence materials for a variety of different departments, such as Admiralty Signals Charts, manuals of aerial reconnaissance photographs and aerial propaganda leaflets, including a daily German newspaper. Like the subject matter it contains — and the man who compiled it — the volume is cloaked in mystery.

It is believed the books were produced for an American mission to Britain in February 1942 under Major General Carl Spaatz. The Americans were keen to learn about British escape and evasion work, and copies of the book were laid on a large mahogany table in a secure space where they could be examined without prying eyes. The United States of America had entered the Second World War following the Japanese attack on Pearl Harbor on 7 December 1941,

A striking oil painting of Lt Gilbert Insall VC, MC, First World War escaper, by Edward Newling, whom IWM commissioned in 1919 to paint the portraits of RAF VC recipients.

Prime Minister Winston Churchill escaped from Boer War captivity in December 1899, without a map and compass. He is on the right-hand side of this POW group, staring directly at the camera in a defiant pose.

and there was close co-operation between M.I.9 and its later American counterpart MIS-X.

It has been estimated that fewer than 20 of these albums were produced. A presentation copy signed by Christopher Clayton Hutton is known to be in Sir Winston Churchill's library at Chartwell. Britain's wartime prime minister had escaped captivity in the Boer War and was a subsequent supporter of the work of M.I.9. In August 1941, he produced a message of hope and encouragement (see page 65) that was sent into camps using the cigar carrier on page 42.

Neither the M.I.9 war diary or war history makes any mention of this volume, or details the occasion for which it was produced. It is possible that similar volumes were to be created to hold escape maps. The British Library has correspondence files from Waddington, the Leeds-based company that manufactured the maps and made *Monopoly* and other games (similar to those shown on page 38) into which these and other aids could be inserted. The documents request a quote for six bright red leather-bound albums for each of four different categories of 'pictures' (their term for maps), but these were to be added to as further work was done, and in this way differ from this very finished and complete volume. There is no indication these were ever produced.

Christopher Clayton Hutton, known as 'Clutty' to his friends, was behind the ingenious

Group photograph of British POW taken at Colditz in December 1940; reply cards are featured in this volume from several of these men, including Lt Col Guy German, Senior British Officer at the time, centre of the middle row, and Capt R H Howe, Escape Officer, 1942–1945, on the right of the front row.

inventions featured in this volume, and is believed to be the creator of this book. His brilliant inventions may have also inspired many of the gadgets created by Q in Ian Fleming's James Bond novels and films. Fleming himself was an influential naval intelligence officer, and some of his many responsibilities included liaising with the different intelligence services. Hutton served with the Yorkshire Regiment and as a pilot with the Royal Air Force (RAF) during the First World War. This was followed by a varied career, working in journalism, publicity and films. He had a long-standing interest in escapology, and in 1913 had challenged Houdini to escape from a wooden packing box on stage at the Birmingham Empire; he lost

the dare and later learned Houdini had bribed the carpenter. His eccentricity, enthusiasm and determined ingenuity were deemed to be a perfect fit for the role of Technical Officer at M.I.9. He was to invent the escape aids, organise their manufacture and devise methods of getting them into camps. Former escaper Air Marshal Sir Basil Embry was an admirer of Hutton and explained he was 'a man of action and ideas... Some people may think he is eccentric; I think he is a genius.' A similar commendation was given by his commanding officer to a provost marshal (an indication of the trouble Hutton frequently found himself in): 'This officer is eccentric. He cannot be expected to comply with ordinary service discipline, but

A photograph of the discovered tunnel at Holzminden, through which 29 POW escaped on the night of 23 July 1918, donated by Captain Brian O'Donoghue Manning who was a prisoner in the camp.

he is far too valuable for his services to be lost to this department.'

Hutton was a skilled publicist, and this album was a way of showcasing the inventions that had been produced and his role in creating them. Sun Engraving printed many consumer magazines, ranging from the pioneering photojournalist *Picture Post* to glossy publications, such as *Vogue*. The exquisite composition and precise design of the book attracts attention and shouts modernity. This is echoed in the crisp Sans Serif font and subtle use of red ink, with the small red circles suggestive of microdot technology, highlighting its secrecy and importance. The single place where other colours are applied is on page 5, where the tri-service M.I.9 constituency is suggested with the traditional shades of dark blue for the navy, red for the army and light blue for the RAF. The tiny RAF roundel below with the light-blue outer ring is not strictly accurate but reflects the importance of these gadgets for the men who would risk their lives most nights when flying over enemy occupied territory. They would shortly be joined by the United States Army Air Forces, who were indirectly the target audience of many of the devices featured in this book. Hutton was a former pilot himself, and the title on the original cover – *Per Ardua Libertas* (*Freedom through Adversity*) – seems to consciously shadow the RAF motto, *Per Ardua Ad Astra* (*Through Adversity to the Stars*).

Established on 23 December 1939, M.I.9 was based for most of the war at Wilton Park, Beaconsfield. It was headed by Major (later Brigadier) Norman Crockatt, who, as a Royal Scots officer, had been decorated in the First World War, and very ably ran this new department and the difficult task of negotiating the hidden intelligence world, together with traditional government bureaucracy and personal politicking. This was compounded by the inter-service rivalries of a tri-service organisation. The Air Ministry had begun formulating plans to assist downed aircrew shortly after the outbreak of the war, while the War Office opposingly believed that thinking about capture was defeatist, and the Admiralty initially ignored it as a possibility.

'Escape-mindedness' was the central philosophy of M.I.9. It sought to provide guidance and physical assistance, ranging from what to expect and how to deal with interrogation to up-to-date information on escape tips, escape lines and aids. It also intended to inspire those who had the misfortune to find themselves behind the lines in hostile territory, keen to avoid capture (evaders) or those in enemy hands or incarcerated in camps (escapers).

The clear message was that it was the duty of anyone in this position to attempt to escape, return to Britain or Allied lines and resume the fight. Everyone was needed in the Total War against Nazi Germany, and later further afield, especially those with valuable experience and technical knowledge, such as pilots and aircrew who underwent lengthy and expensive training. Even if an escape was unsuccessful, it should not be regarded as a failure as it could provide essential experience and useful information that could be passed back to British authorities. It also occupied their captors, tied up enemy manpower and kept them out of the fight. The morale effect of a known missing person reappearing was phenomenal – M.I.9 would make use of recently returned escapers and evaders to inspire and share current experience.

The Swiss doctor Adolf Lukas Vischer

'Armour' Tongue tin containing smuggled escape aids sent to Major Jack W Shaw at Holzminden by his mother. The tin had been opened and resealed with its contents substituted with five compasses, two wire-cutters and maps, as well as a piece of lead to ensure the sealed tin matched the weight on the label.

coined the phrase 'Barbed Wire Disease' as a result of his research into the detrimental mental impact of captivity on First World War POW. Escape-mindedness would mitigate this, instilling a sense of purpose, interest and alertness. It would ensure POW were still able to contribute to the war effort from the unique position of being behind enemy lines.

This volume demonstrates the material assistance M.I.9 provided, issued either pre-operationally or sent to escape committees in prison camps. It only covers the early part of the war, and thus concentrates on escapes from Germany. It is ironic that it covers the period up to 14 February 1942. The following day would

see the Fall of Singapore, and the capture of well over 60,000 British and Commonwealth POW (precise numbers are subject to debate and impossible to state with certainty). The Far East Prisoner of War situation would prove much more challenging, although M.I.9 was still operational there.

First World War experience was highly valued within M.I.9, and both the RAF and Royal Navy had representatives who had been POW in that war. Alfred John 'Johnny' Evans was a former RAF officer, whose exemplary escaping experiences from both German and Turkish captivity were detailed in his phenomenally successful book *The Escaping Club*. This book

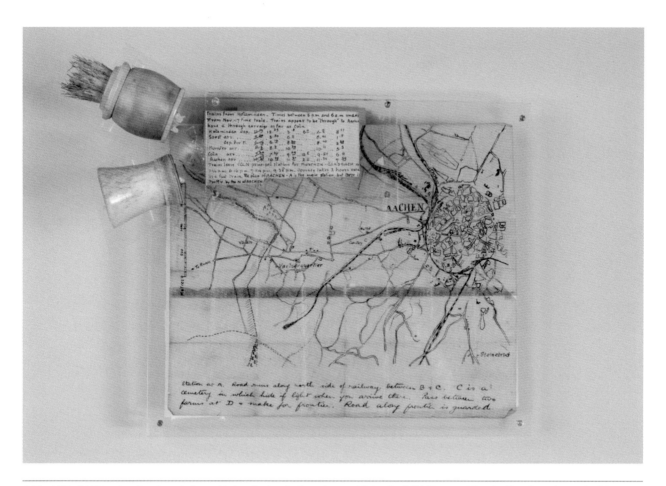

A First World War shaving brush from Holzminden belonging to Major Jack W Shaw, with a hollow interior to hold a map of Aachen and environs, and a railway timetable, which has parallels with the ingenious devices produced by M.I.9.

could be regarded as an escaper's manual — it was full of tips such as carrying black pepper to prevent dogs picking up your scent and walking along railway tracks in unfamiliar territory to avoid getting lost. It was to inspire the next generation who found themselves in similar situations. He also highlighted the important role of experience and knowledge. His family had endured the agony of not knowing the fate of a loved one, when his brother Ralph was reported missing at Ypres, Belgium, in April 1915. The long delay in hearing he was safe but in captivity, ensured Evans, a pilot in the Royal Flying Corps (RFC), made provision for the distinct possibility that he might find himself

in similar circumstances. He and his mother devised a secret code, which meant he could communicate with her — and she was to supply him with all manner of escape aids, ranging from maps baked in cakes to compasses hidden in jars of prunes and anchovy paste.

One of the first things M.I.9 did on 29 December 1939 was engage former First World War POW as lecturers. On 5 January 1940, an outline address was delivered by Evans at a conference in which former inmates of Holzminden participated. This camp had been the scene of the greatest breakout of that war, when 29 men escaped through a tunnel on the night of 23 July 1918, with 10 successful home

Captain Gilbert Insall, VC, wearing his escaping kit – note his pilot's wings on the inside of his reversed jacket.

paperwork and led to further fear and suspicion. The Germans were wise to the tricks employed by POW and had absorbed many of the 'escape' manuals and memoirs published in the inter-war period. The British consequently had to be one step ahead every time a new aid or hiding place was discovered.

However, a map and compass were still regarded as the key requirements, and these would be the initial aids that Hutton worked on. Knowledge about their importance, and recommended hiding places, had developed during the First World War. An official lecture to aircrew in the latter part of 1918 suggested hiding maps 'In lining of flying coat, Under leather on inside of riding breeches, In lining on shoulder of tunic, Under cuff of tunic, In lining of flying boot (probably best of all)', while a compass could be secreted 'In heel of flying boot, Countersunk into button of tunic, Under metal star or shoulder strap, Under cloth star on cuff of tunic.' IWM has examples of maps and escape aids smuggled into camps – with those belonging to Major Jack W Straw being particularly fine specimens because they were not used. He was 31st in the queue to get out of the tunnel at Holzminden, but it collapsed after 29 escaped.

On starting his work, Hutton was advised to look back at the First World War, and he began by visiting the 'British Museum's extensive library' for advice on POW book titles, around 50 of which he then sourced from second-hand book shops.

He does not mention the Imperial War Museum, so it is unclear whether he sought assistance here. It would have been negligent not to have approached the institution as, alongside volumes in the museum's library, he would have been able to actually see and

runs. As the war progressed more lecturers were added, including many who had authored Great War escape accounts, as well as 'This War Escapers' who shared up-to-date experiences.

Evans believed that escaping in the Second World War was much more difficult than in the First. Far more of Europe was hostile territory, resulting in longer, more treacherous treks to freedom. There were more purpose-built hutted POW camps, which were arguably harder to break free from. And the Gestapo's grip on Germany ensured greater control over movement and instigated tightened searches; this put a great strain on having up-to-date

An early IWM display case showing 'relics of Lieutenant Gilbert Insall'. The grey wool cloth lining sewn into the inside of his service jacket can clearly be seen, together with other items used in escape attempts.

and Insall explained to Evans, 'gear connected with escapes is always interesting, and I hope to have quite a good little corner devoted to P. of W. (RAF).' Evans was reluctant to part with his 'wrist compass & maps, which were smuggled to me from England, some filthy clothes, German boots and Tyrolese hat' and was incredulous that they could be of interest to the general public.

Insall had a better response from other escapers, not least his own brother Gilbert Insall, who as well as being a Victoria Cross (VC) winner, effected a dramatic escape from Ströhen camp in the company of Captain Michael Harrison and Captain Claude Templer on the night of 23 August 1917. They had dug a hole and hid underneath the floor of the bathroom hut, which was outside the main confines of the camp and only used by POW in the morning with brief disturbances by the odd German guard looking for soap remnants. They surfaced at 2am and then set off on their 130-kilometre and 9-night trek to neutral Holland. The M.I.9 suit disguise on page 47 had a precedent with the grey wool cloth lining of Insall's RFC tunic – he wore it reversed to resemble a civilian jacket.

Lawrence Arthur Wingfield, captured on 1 July 1916, following a successful raid on Saint-Quentin railway station, France, recorded that it was only when he reached his fifth and final prison camp that he really thought about escaping. The enthusiasm for escaping within Ströhen was infectious, and he specifically commented that Insall's successful escape 'inspired me to have a go'. IWM has the notes Wingfield used as an M.I.9 lecturer, as well as escape maps and his service headgear which he transformed into a flat cap for his 'home run' in October 1917. He compares the differences

examine escape aids which had been used during the war. Evans knew that IWM had this material as he had been contacted on 19 September 1919 by Algernon John Insall, who had been tasked with acquiring RAF material for the newly established museum. Insall was keen to collect as many objects as possible showing the wide range and development of the recently formed aviation branch of the armed forces. The POW experience had been rather overlooked by the initial collecting committees that set up IWM,

Portrait of Major Christopher Clayton Hutton, c.1944. He is wearing his army uniform with First World War campaign medal ribbons, RAF pilot's wings and Intelligence Corps cap and lapel badges.

between the prisoners of both conflicts. He believed First World War POW were unaware of military intelligence, failed to escape due to their selfish attitudes and ignorance and ultimately lacked help and effective planning. He stressed that failure had a value, and that the modern POW had a duty to escape, to find out information and to either transmit it or bring it back home.

The transmission of information to and from prison camps became widespread and sophisticated. Broader information of military importance, such as troop movements, war damage or industrial details, could be sent to British intelligence, while camp escape committees could request items they needed and sound the alarm when escape aids had been discovered and should no longer be sent. M.I.9 could let the camps know about successful escapes and provide up-to-date information about routes, stamps, documents and operational messages. M.I.9 trained selected men to communicate in code and ran a programme of bogus letter-writers to correspond with those who had the misfortune to be captured. This album shows wireless receivers sent into camps on pages 66–67, through which POW could receive the BBC broadcast programme *Radio Padre*, featuring the Reverend Ronald Selby Wright, and if it began with 'Good Evening Forces' a coded message was included for their benefit.

Having produced the escape gadgets, smuggling them into camps was the next step to be organised and co-ordinated. This book beautifully reveals how this was done; M.I.9 did not want to compromise morale-boosting Red Cross or personal parcels and would not use food as a carrier because they knew how essential it would be to POW. Instead, they invented a variety of welfare organisations to send games and clothing as gifts. The first of these was the Prisoners' Leisure Hours Fund, based at a real bombed-out address, with clues in their organisational stationery that must have raised smiles for both those inventing and receiving it: 'Bolt Court', 'Fleet Street', the Bunyanesque homily – 'The treasures to be found in idle hours – only those who seek may find' by 'Runyon', with prominent names including 'Miss Freda Mappin' and 'The Hon Mrs E Freeman'.

The book incorporates the actual reply cards returned to M.I.9, and we can see how the parcels have been numbered, with the contents detailed, dated and signed for by the recipients. The reply cards were slightly larger than those of the Red Cross to enable the censors to identify them quickly and send them on to M.I.9 as soon as possible. The front and back of the cards can be synchronised by matching the potentially mysterious letter that appears on opposite pages. Many of these responses came from Oflag IVC – better known as Colditz – with Lt Col Guy German, the Senior British Officer there at the time, having sent back cards on pages 53 and 60–61. The latter replies relate to the parcels sent by the fictitious 'Reverend C O Verall' who was sending out the surviving books from his bombed-out vicarage – maps and money could duly be discovered under the endpapers (page 42). When these were 'blown', Hutton moved on to hiding the same items in gramophone records (which he nicknamed 'Operation Smash-Hit'), of chiefly popular composers such as Beethoven and Wagner (page 43).

Hutton actively worked for M.I.9 for a period of three years, and this album marks the first two years of his service. He himself

In an era of rationing and shortages, M.I.9 silk escape maps were popular purchases on the open market following the end of the war. This dressing gown is made from escape maps of South East Asia.

gave varying dates for the time he was with the organisation (and each was suspiciously symmetrical) – either between 14 February 1940 to 14 February 1943, or 5 February 1940 to 5 February 1943. No doubt the exhausting hard work of these years contributed to his subsequent hospitalisation in Woodside Officers Hospital, North London, which specialised in treating mental health conditions. He was invalided out of the army in November 1944, and a later application to join the Special Operations Executive was unsuccessful. From December that year, he served as a civilian with the RAF at the Central Interpretation Unit at Medmenham.

Yet his M.I.9 work was obviously extremely important to him. He had been with the organisation from the start, had been at the forefront of ingenious design and initiated the way in which escape gadgets were smuggled into camps. As M.I.9 grew, the organisation became more complex and other prominent names, such as Charles Fraser-Smith and Jasper Maskelyne, became involved in a similar capacity. This album leaves a record of Hutton's work and charts the progression of escape technology.

Money and recognition appear to have been Hutton's chief motivations in wanting to write and lecture after the war on his M.I.9 work, and problems quickly arose. He had signed the Official Secrets Act, and with the rapid onset of the Cold War and the start of the Korean War in 1950, there was still a considerable sensitivity around M.I.9's creations. Former POW may have published accounts of their own experiences, but Hutton would be disclosing the whole story to the public from an internal War Office viewpoint. In 1960 he successfully published *Official Secret: The Remarkable Story of Escape*

Aids — Their Invention, Production — And The Sequel. The memoir describes his wartime story and its aftermath in selective and dramatic terms. It makes absolutely no mention of this volume, or the 1942 American visit. Barbara Bond has since shown he lacked understanding of military mapping, and that silk maps were not a novel invention but were used by the Chinese as early as the second century BC, while cloth maps were used in the American Civil War.

Hutton had been trying to publish and talk about his M.I.9 experiences for well over a decade before 1960, and there had been litigation over several previous publications.

Although the War Office had given him permission to speak about the general history of escaping in 50 different stories (none dating later than 1934), an American lecture tour caused complaints from the United States Air Force in 1951 due to the classified information he was speaking sensationally and publicly about. He was subsequently summoned and ordered to hand over confidential material that he should not have had in his possession; the first item of which was a 'volume bound in red leather, and containing coloured illustrations of the processes for production of M.I.9 equipment, including compasses, maps, and other devices' — likely a copy of this very book.

The case was ultimately dropped. Hutton was also able to show that all the objects he referenced were already in the public domain, including a fly button compass, tunic button compass and a silk map that had been on show at IWM since 1947. In view of this revelation, the Air Ministry requested their removal from display in December 1952 and provided a blown tropical survival pack as a substitute to replace the empty space. There was no criticism of IWM here as the Air Ministry had sent the items in the first place, and Hutton's comments about most of these items being publicly available were factual as the Ministry of Supply was selling off escape devices such as compasses and flying boots. Silk maps were very popular items to purchase at a time of clothes rationing too, and IWM has several garments created from these delicate but vital former escape aids.

Hutton died in Ashburton, Devon, and his gravestone shows what he clearly considered to be the highlight of an eventful life, reading 'Christopher William Clayton Hutton: Major, M.I.9, 1939–45: whose escape devices aided so many prisoners of war: Died 3rd September 1965: Aged 71 years'.

Despite Hutton's early exit from M.I.9 in 1943, the organisation evolved and grew as the war progressed, but as with virtually everything that happened in the Second World War, this had a firm precedent with the 1914–1918 experience. It strove for the most up-to-date escape information to share with the men who needed it and to warn against previously issued advice or aids that had been compromised. The service continually developed and finetuned the items they produced. More than 35,000 escapers and evaders returned to fight another day — no doubt with the help of many of the escape aids found within this book. ●

Sarah Paterson
IWM Curator

PART TWO

MOST SECRET

THE FUNCTIONS OF M.I.9
WERE GOVERNED BY A
CHARTER TO SERVE ═══

───── THE NAVY ─────

───── THE ARMY ─────

THE ROYAL AIR FORCE

M. I. 9
TECHNICAL

WAR OFFICE
LONDON
S.W.1

War Office,

London, S.W.1.

14.2.1942.

NOTE.

The following pages give a photographic review of the range of work I was privileged to be entrusted with on behalf of Section M.I.9, for two years between February 14th, 1940, and February 14th, 1942.

They show "Aids to Escape" - Pre-Capture and Post-Capture - and in addition show various other articles called for by various Sections of the three Services which, through the channels laid on, M.I.9, were enabled to produce or deliver quickly.

No details are given in this review of the difficulties experienced in obtaining manufacture of the various Aids. These are dealt with in separate notes—as are the names of the manufacturers.

Two points, perhaps, should be put on record. During the period covered, no finished working suggestion was ever submitted to me by any other Service Department and no Service Factory or Organisation was used in the manufacture of any article.

I should like to record my sincere thanks to Colonel N. R. Crockatt, D.S.O., M.C., for his kindly understanding of the very difficult problems with which I was faced and for the considerable latitude he has always granted me in letting me work in my own irregular way; without such help the results shown in this book could never have been so effectively achieved.

With but few exceptions, all articles were devised and production obtained by me.

C. Clayton Hutton

Major.

The Charter.

CONDUCT OF WORK No. 48.
M.I.9.

1.   A new section of the Intelligence Directorate at the War Office has been formed. It will be called M.I.9. It will work in close connection with and act as agent for the Admiralty and Air Ministry.

2.   The Section is responsible for:—

   (a) The preparation and *execution* of plans for facilitating the escape of British Prisoners of War of all three Services in Germany or elsewhere.

   (b) Arranging instruction in connection with above.

   (c) Making other advance provision, as considered necessary.

   (d) Collection and dissemination of information obtained from British Prisoners of War.

   (e) Advising on counter-escape measures for German Prisoners of War in Great Britain, if requested to do so.

3.   M.I.9. will be accommodated in Room 424, Metropole Hotel.

(Sgd.)   J. SPENCER.

Col. G.S.

23.12.39.   for D.M.I.

On February 14th 1941 the Commissioned Staff
of M.I.9 consisted of:

COLONEL N. R. CROCKATT, D.S.O., M.C.

MAJOR V. A. R. ISHAM, M.C.   MAJOR C. M. RAIT, M.C.

SQDN. LEADER A. J. EVANS, M.C.   COMMANDER P. W. RHODES, R.N.

MAJOR C. CLAYTON HUTTON
(TECHNICAL)

●

OPERATIONS WERE CONDUCTED FROM THE
WAR OFFICE   LONDON, S.W.I.

●

MAPS

After exhaustive tests to find a material that would be waterproof, subject to the smallest printing and confinable in the smallest space, a special type of silk was used.

At first this material was printed on one side only, but it was found that by special treatment maps could be printed on both sides of it.

Later on, artificial silk was similarly treated and used as well.

Up to February 14th, 1942, 56 maps were produced covering every theatre of war as the following lists show.

Portions of some printed specimens on double-sided and one-sided silk are shown on pages 20—23.

THE FOLLOWING MAPS WERE PRINTED ON ONE-SIDED SILK AND ON PAPER.

Germany (5 *kinds*).

North France (2 *kinds*).

South France (2 *kinds*).

England and North France.

Norway and Sweden (2 *kinds*).

Norway.

Sweden.

Spain.

Spain, Portugal and Corsica.

North Italy (2 *kinds*).

South Italy (2 *kinds*).

Cyrenaica.

Eritrea.

Abyssinia.

Somaliland.

Juba River.

Roumania and Bulgaria (2 *kinds*).

Russia.

North West Russia, Poland, Finland.

Greece and Jugoslavia (2 *kinds*).

Turkey.

Caucasus.

Syria and Iraq.

Persia.

Middle East.

Iran.

Spittal (*route*).

Basle (*route*).

South Germany (*route*).

Schaffhausen (*route*) (2 *kinds*).

Baltic (*route*).

Brussels (3 *parts*).

MAPS

THE FOLLOWING MAPS WERE PRINTED ON
DOUBLE-SIDED SILK AND ON PAPER.

Germany / North France.

Germany / North France and England.

Germany / Norway and Sweden.

North France / South France.

South France / Spain.

South France / Spain, Portugal, and Corsica.

Norway / Sweden.

Spain, Portugal, Corsica / North West African Coast.

North Italy / South Italy.

South Italy / Cyrenaica.

Cyrenaica / Middle East.

Morocco, Tripoli / North West African Coast.

Cyrenaica / Morocco, Tripoli.

North West African Coast, both sides.

West African Coast, both sides.

Eritrea / Abyssinia.

Roumania, Bulgaria / Greece and Jugoslavia.

Roumania, Bulgaria / Russia

Roumania, Bulgaria / Middle East.

Russia / North West Russia, Poland, Finland.

Greece and Crete / Italy, Greece, Turkey in Europe.

Turkey / Syria, Iraq.

Caucasus / Persia.

Middle East / Iran.

Spittal / Basle.

209,000
MAPS

AND

214,000
AIDS ITEMS

FOR

PRE AND POST CAPTURE

WERE DISTRIBUTED
UP TO FEBRUARY 14th, 1942
TO UNITS OF THE THREE SERVICES

MAKING A TOTAL OF

423,000
AIDS

Map of Germany printed in three colours on silk.

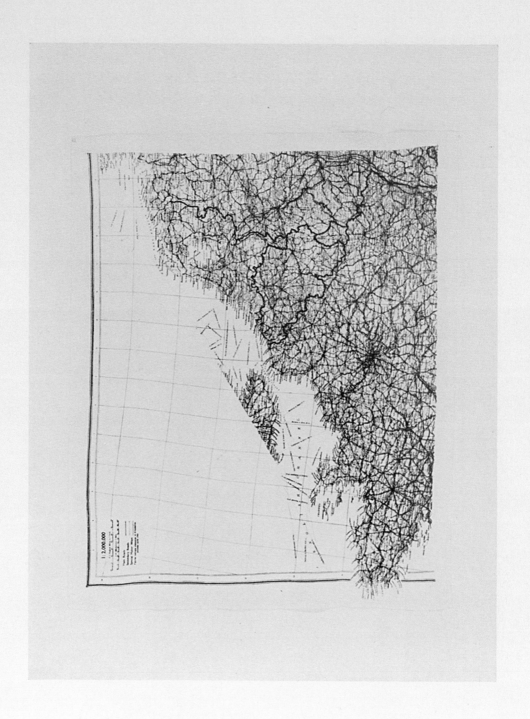

Map of N. France printed in three colours on silk.

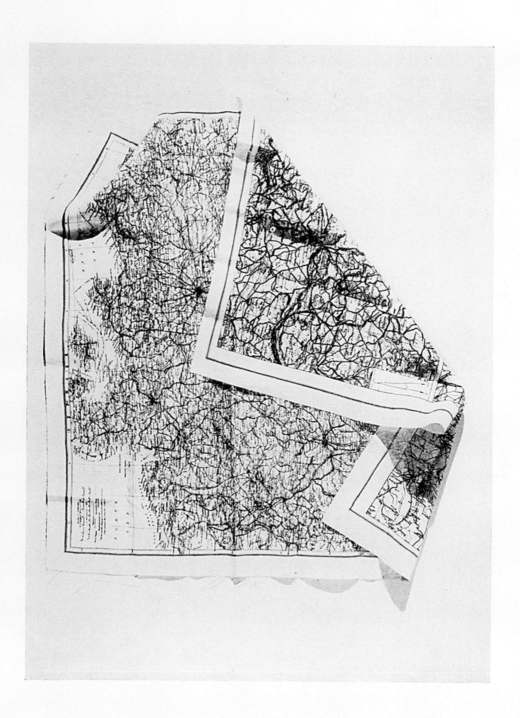

Map of Germany in three colours on one side of the silk and
Map of certain German border districts in three colours on reverse.

Spittal Route Map printed in four colours on tissue.

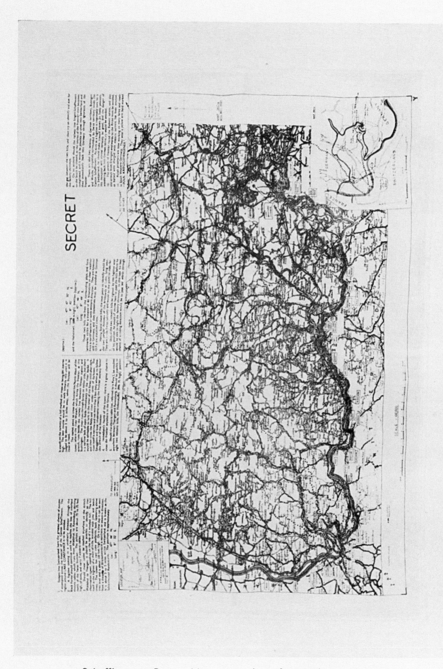

Schaffhausen Route Map printed in four colours on tissue.

SILK MAPS

Single-sided

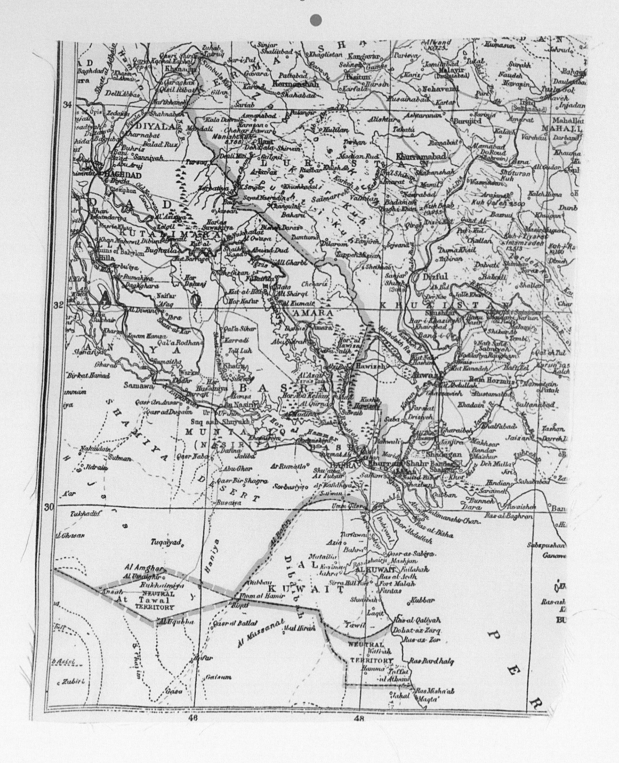

SILK MAPS

Double-sided

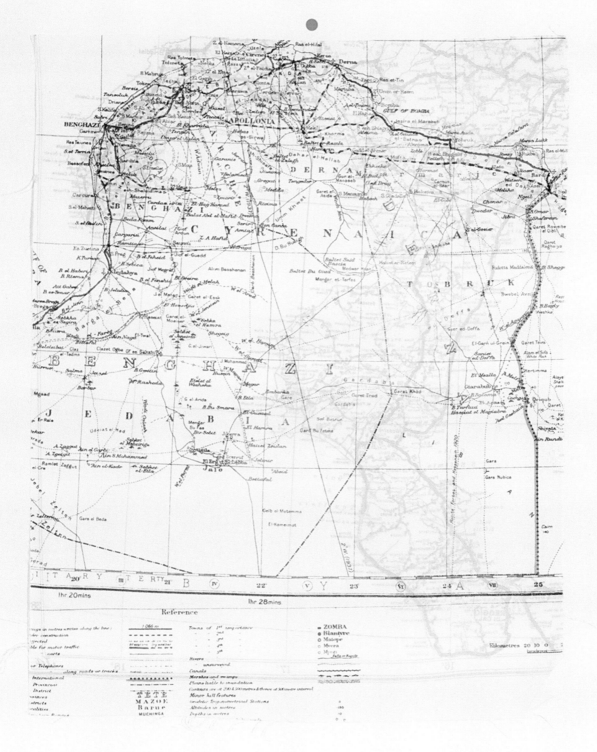

ARTIFICIAL SILK MAPS

(Waterproofed 'Tenasco')

Double-sided

TISSUE MAPS

One-sided only

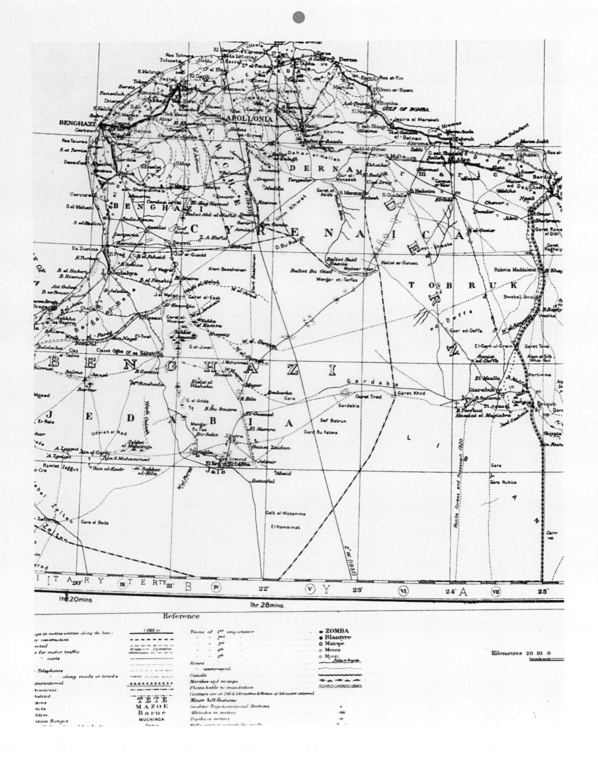

A STANDARD ROTOR WAS EVOLVED WHICH COULD BE INTERCHANGED IN VARIOUS ARTICLES.

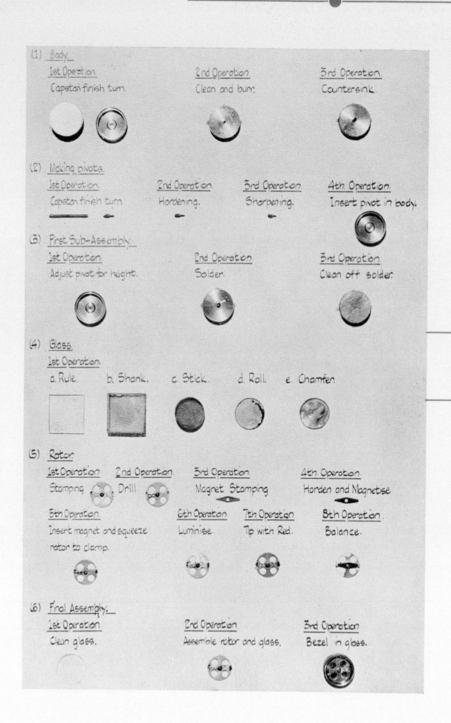

This is photographic lay-out showing complete operation from the raw material to the finished round compass.

STANDARD COMPASSES
photographed half size larger
than actual.

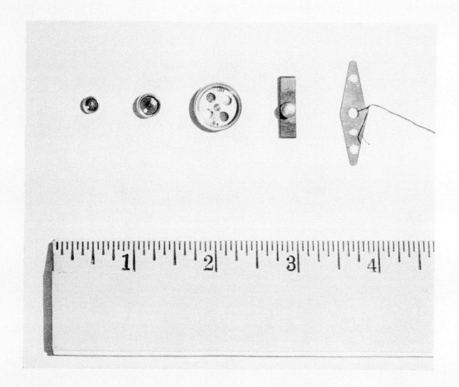

Several types of Compasses were designed, but those most
used consisted of various sizes of
Luminous Rotating
Hanging Swinging
Balancing Swinging

STANDARD R.A.F. BUTTON LUMINOUS COMPASS.

Same design applied to all Service Buttons.

STANDARD WOOLWORTH LUMINOUS STUD COMPASS

ORDINARY BRASS SERVICE FLY BUTTON.   (In pairs.)

One Button swings on top of the other, pointing due north.
Luminous.

FOUNTAIN PEN COMPASS

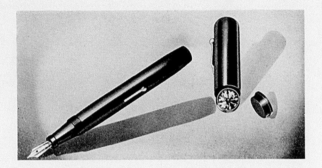

Various types of this were used.

PIPE

This contained compass and also a chemical substance.

RATION BOX. I.

(Size $5\frac{3}{4}'' \times 4\frac{1}{4}'' \times \frac{7}{8}''$)

●

This Ration Box is in a 50 'Players' Cigarette Tin.

●

Of this model and model 2 there were supplied up to February 14th, 1942 — 23,800

●

Contents.

1. Rubber Water Bottle.
2. Horlicks Tablets.
3. Packet of Benzedrine Drugs.
4. Packet of Halazone Water Softener.
5. Packet of Chewing Gum.
6. Bar of Chocolate.
7. Box of Matches.

●

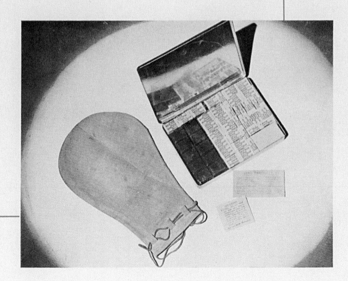

RATION BOX. 2.

(Size 6″ x 4¼″ x 1″)

●

This Ration Box is made of Acetate.

●

It is transparent and watertight.

●

Contents.

1. Rubber Water Bottle.
2. Horlicks Tablets.
3. Packet of Benzedrine Drugs.
4. Packet of Halazone Water Softener.
5. Packet of Chewing Gum.
6. Bar of Chocolate.
7. Box of Matches.
8. Two Tubes Condensed Milk.
9. Saw.
10. Compass.

●

(In some instances special Maps were also included).

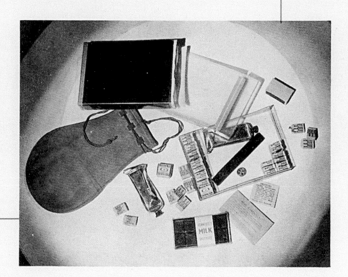

HACK-SAW

Hack-saw supplied with straight handle.

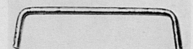

Handle bends at given points.

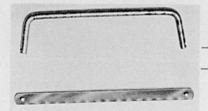

Saw springs into frame.

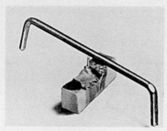

Handle magnetized to swing due North.

RAZOR BLADES

All types were used. Only one blade in each packet magnetized.

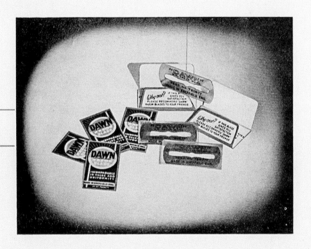

Clipping from Blade centre also magnetized.

OFFICER'S HAT SUPPORT.

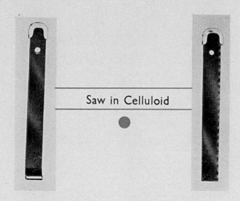

Saw in Celluloid

Fastest and steadiest way of resting Blade and Swinger Compasses — in water.

STANDARD SIZE PENCILS.

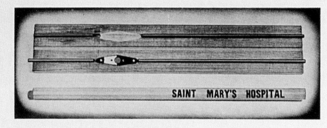

PENCIL CONCEALING SWINGER.

PENCIL CONCEALING THIN SAW IN LEAD ITSELF.

PENCIL CLIP
COMPASS.

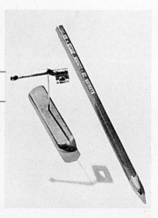

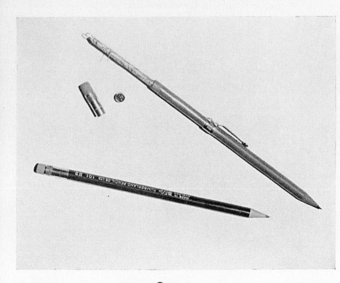

Contents

| 1 Map | 1 Compass (Luminous) | 1 Pencil Clip Compass |

STANDARD EVERSHARP PENCIL REFILLS.
One steel lead Compass Needle in each box.

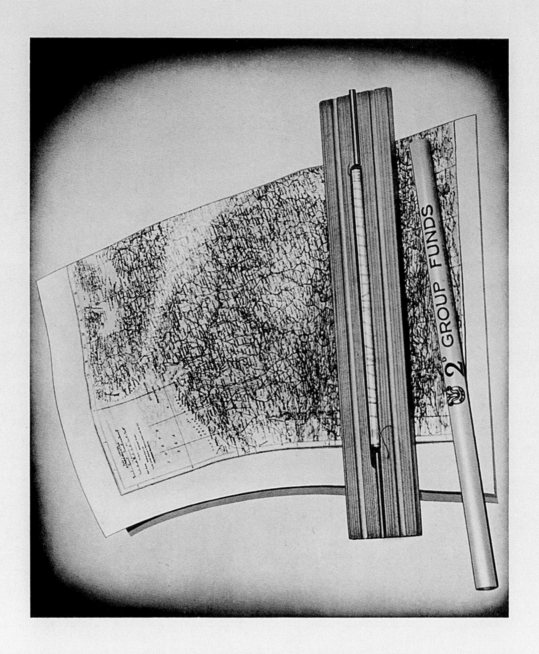

PENCIL CONCEALING ROLLED TISSUE MAP

SPECIAL R.A.F. BOOT.

Boot designed to fit snugly round leg and foot. In boot strap is Knife. By cutting round seam, top part comes away — leaving perfect walking shoe.

GAMES CARRIERS AND THEIR CONTENTS.

(Maps and various escape aids)

SMALL CHESS SET.

CRIBBAGE BOARD.

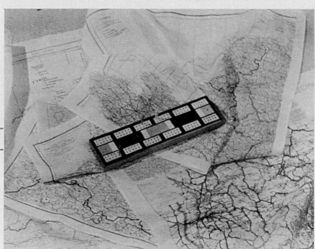

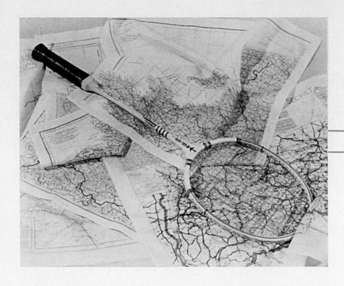

SQUASH RACKET.

GAMES CARRIERS AND THEIR CONTENTS.

(Maps and various escape aids)

MEDIUM CHESS SET.

BACKGAMMON SET.

LARGE CHESS SET.

GAMES CARRIERS AND THEIR CONTENTS.

(Maps and various escape aids).

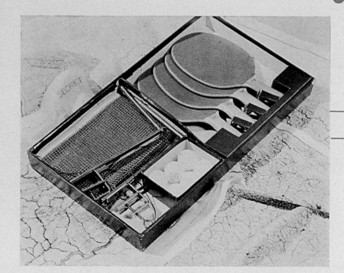

TABLE TENNIS SET.

DRAUGHTS BOARD.

DOMINOES SET.

GAMES CARRIERS.

DARTBOARD.

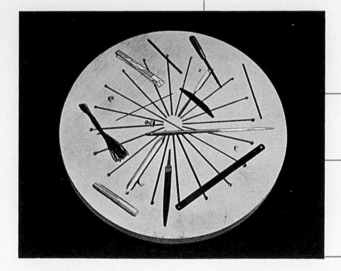

Each game was made by hand by the finest craftsmen, containing various escape aids.

"Doves" were used as well.

WOODEN CARRIERS.

Various wooden carriers used.

All were made by hand by the finest
craftsmen, all elderly men. They were
all non subject to X-Ray.

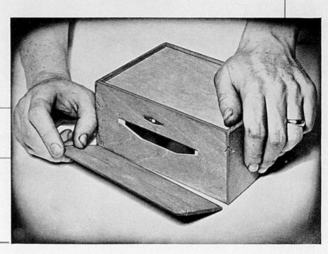

TOILET SET CARRIERS AND THEIR CONTENTS.

(Maps and various escape aids).

MISCELLANEOUS CARRIERS.

STANDARD PACK OF PLAYING CARDS.

Each pack is one Map. 48 Cards covered a Map. The 4 Aces are a small Map of Europe. The Joker is the Key. The outside Card contains the instructions.

CIGAR CARRIER.

Contains either tissue or silk map and compass.

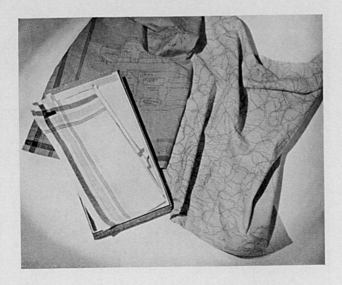

STANDARD COTTON HANDKERCHIEFS.

(Result obtained when washed with chemical on page 65.)

NEW AND SECOND HAND BOOK CARRIER.

MISCELLANEOUS CARRIERS

TOOTH — GOLD FITTING made to measure

Small medium luminous compass fits in jaws on left and thin gold tube holding message or map slides on to the two prongs at bottom.   These are concealed through being in between the cheek and gum.

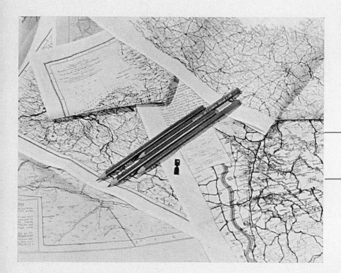

BRIDGE MARKER PENCILS
AND THEIR CONTENTS.

STANDARD SANDALS
which were asked for under the name
of "Picer" model.
(*Pice being Indian currency.*)

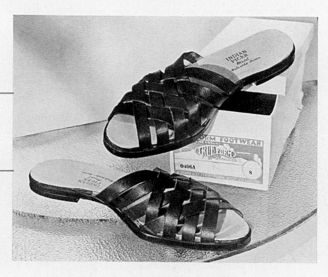

GRAMOPHONE RECORD CARRIER.

This is a standard record and contents were secreted in *both* sides.   The record was perfect in every way and could be played.

STANDARD "HALEX" TOILET GOODS.

Containing Maps, Saws and Compasses.

BABY TELESCOPE

Magnification 8 and 6.
For watching guards, etc.

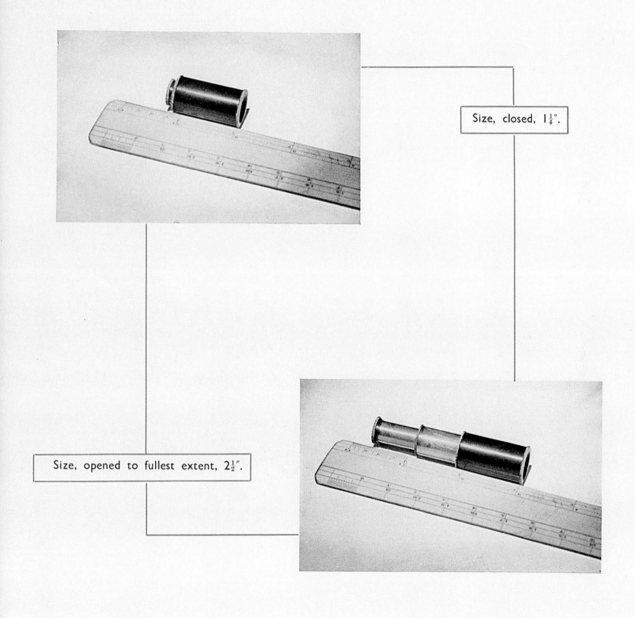

Size, closed, $1\frac{1}{4}''$.

Size, opened to fullest extent, $2\frac{1}{2}''$.

SPECIAL MESS DRESS.

In one minute a perfect
fitting walking out suit
can be made — which
is also waterproofed.

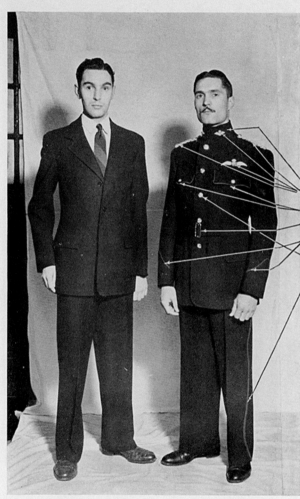

Take out Buckram
Take off Badges
Tear off Pockets & Flaps
Take off Belt
Tear off Sleeve Piping
Buttons replaced by those
from inside Trouser Tops
Tear off Stripes

TWO-WAY R.A.F. SUIT

Officers and O/R's.

Turned inside-out, a perfect
walking out suit is made.

POST CAPTURE

AIDS

WERE PACKED AND DESPATCHED
TO THE VARIOUS P/W CAMPS

●

THE NAMES AND ADDRESSES OF ASSOCIATIONS,
SOCIETIES AND NUMEROUS PRIVATE INDIVIDUALS,
ALL OF WHICH WERE FICTITIOUS, WERE USED IN
EVERY INSTANCE, SOME OF WHICH ARE GIVEN ON
THE FOLLOWING PAGES

●

ALL THESE WERE, IN FACT,

M.I.9

———————————●———————————

"Good" parcels and "Naughty" parcels ready for despatch.

●

PRISONERS' LEISURE HOURS FUND

*" The treasures to be found in idle hours—
only those who seek may find."*
Runyan.

President :
B. ATTENBOROUGH, Esq.

.

Vice-Presidents :
Sir THOMAS BERNEY, Bart.
L. C. UNDERHILL, Esq.

.

Committee :
Lady D. BROWNE.
The Hon. Mrs. E. FREEMAN.
P. O. NORTON, Esq.
J. B. WORLES, Esq.

**66 BOLT COURT,
FLEET STREET,
LONDON, E.C.4.**

Hon. Treasurer :
E. TOWNSEND, Esq., C.A.

.

Hon. Secretary :
Miss FREDA MAPPIN.

.

Telephone :
CENTRAL 3951

12th MAY, 1941

Dear Sir,

     Through the kindness of one of our
contributors, we are enabled to send to you a
selection of Musical Instruments - and Gramophone
Records, and we are having despatched direct from the
manufacturers in the course of a few days some records.

     We intend despatching different selections
for each prisoner of war - to whom we send these, and
it is hoped in order that all may enjoy the variety,
you will offer to interchange with each other.

     Further supplies will be sent you at regular
intervals, and if there is any particular record you
desire sent, perhaps you will look through the Catalogues
we are sending letting us know the make and number, and
we will do our best to despatch to you in due course.

     Trusting you are enjoying good health, and
looking on the bright side of things.

     Yours faithfully,

     Secretary.

A Voluntary Fund formed for the purpose of sending Comforts, Games, Books, etc. to British Prisoners of War.

●

LICENSED VICTUALLERS SPORTS

———— ASSOCIATION ————

(WHOLESALE ONLY)

Telephone :
CENTRAL 6952

10, St. BRIDE STREET,
LONDON, E.C.4.

Secretary :
J. H. SHERWELL

Suppliers of Games and Bar Requisites to Hotels, Restaurants, Sports Clubs and other Licensed Premises.

ACKNOWLEDGEMENTS

KRIEGSGEFANGENENPOST

The Hon. Secretary,
PRISONERS' LEISURE HOURS FUND,
66 BOLT COURT,
FLEET STREET,
LONDON, E.C.4.
ENGLAND.

KRIEGSGEFANGENENPOST

The Hon. Secretary,
PRISONERS' LEISURE HOURS FUND,
66 BOLT COURT,
FLEET STREET,
LONDON, E.C.4.
ENGLAND.

KRIEGSGEFANGENENPOST

The Hon. Secretary,
PRISONERS' LEISURE HOURS FUND,
66 BOLT COURT,
FLEET STREET,
LONDON, E.C.4.
ENGLAND.

KRIEGSGEFANGENENPOST

The Hon. Secretary,
PRISONERS' LEISURE HOURS FUND,
66 BOLT COURT,
FLEET STREET,
LONDON, E.C.4.
ENGLAND.

KRIEGSGEFANGENENPOST

The Hon. Secretary,
PRISONERS' LEISURE HOURS FUND,
66 BOLT COURT,
FLEET STREET,
LONDON, E.C.4.
ENGLAND.

KRIEGSGEFANGENENPOST

The Hon. Secretary,
PRISONERS' LEISURE HOURS FUND,
66 BOLT COURT,
FLEET STREET,
LONDON, E.C.4.
ENGLAND.

KRIEGSGEFANGENENPOST

The Hon. Secretary,
PRISONERS' LEISURE HOURS FUND,
66 BOLT COURT,
FLEET STREET,
LONDON, E.C.4.
ENGLAND.

KRIEGSGEFANGENENPOST

The Hon. Secretary,
PRISONERS' LEISURE HOURS FUND,
66 BOLT COURT,
FLEET STREET,
LONDON, E.C.4.
ENGLAND.

In order to test the receipt of parcels, a special card was inserted in each parcel, with a request in the accompanying letter that the German Camp Commandant would be good enough to allow this card to be returned — thus saving a weekly P/W letter.

Nearly all were returned.

A

52

ACKNOWLEDGEMENTS

To
The Hon. Secretary,
PRISONERS' LEISURE HOURS FUND,
66 BOLT COURT, FLEET STREET,
LONDON, E.C.4, ENGLAND.

Date *August 21. 1941.*

Parcel No. *703* Containing:

2 Prs Sox
2 Pr Pants
2 Vests
1 Jersey
1 Pr Boots

has been received by me. *Very many thanks*

(Signed) *A M Allan 2/Lt.*
C/O The 1155

To
The Hon. Secretary,
PRISONERS' LEISURE HOURS FUND,
66 BOLT COURT, FLEET STREET,
LONDON, E.C.4, ENGLAND

Date *July 16*

Parcel No. *707* Containing:

2 Prs of Socks
2 Prs Pants
2 Vests
1 Jersey
1 Pr Boots

has been received by me.

(Signed) *Bury*
Capt

To
The Hon. Secretary,
PRISONERS' LEISURE HOURS FUND,
66 BOLT COURT, FLEET STREET,
LONDON, E.C.4, ENGLAND.

Date

Parcel No. *703* Containing:

2 Prs Socks
2 Pants
2 Vests
1 Jersey
1 Pr Boots

has been received by me.

(Signed)
Oflag XIIC

To
The Hon. Secretary,
PRISONERS' LEISURE HOURS FUND,
66 BOLT COURT, FLEET STREET,
LONDON, E.C.4, ENGLAND.

Date *July 21st 1941.*

Parcel No. *702* Containing:

2 prs. Sox.
2 prs. Pants.
2 Vests.
1 Jersey.
1 pr. Boots.

has been received by me.

(Signed) *Heathonsidon.*
Oflag VA.

To
The Hon. Secretary,
PRISONERS' LEISURE HOURS FUND,
66 BOLT COURT, FLEET STREET,
LONDON, E.C.4, ENGLAND.

Date *12.1/41*

Parcel No. *701* Containing:

has been received by me.

(Signed)

To
The Hon. Secretary,
PRISONERS' LEISURE HOURS FUND,
66 BOLT COURT, FLEET STREET,
LONDON, E.C.4, ENGLAND.

Date *15 July, 41*

Parcel No. *704* Containing:

2/prs Sox
2/pr Pants
2 Vests
1 Jersey
1 Pr Boots

has been received by me.

(Signed) *H Herman Lt.C*

To
The Hon. Secretary,
PRISONERS' LEISURE HOURS FUND,
66 BOLT COURT, FLEET STREET,
LONDON, E.C.4, ENGLAND.

Date *15 JULY*

Parcel No. *706* Containing:

has been received by me.

(Signed)

To
The Hon. Secretary,
PRISONERS' LEISURE HOURS FUND,
66 BOLT COURT, FLEET STREET,
LONDON, E.C.4, ENGLAND.

Date *4 July*

Parcel No. *709* Containing:

2 Prs Sox
2 Prs Pants
2 Vests
1 Jersey
1 Pr Boots

has been received by me.

(Signed)

Acknowledgements of "Dove" parcels which were always sent before "naughty" parcels.

ACKNOWLEDGEMENTS

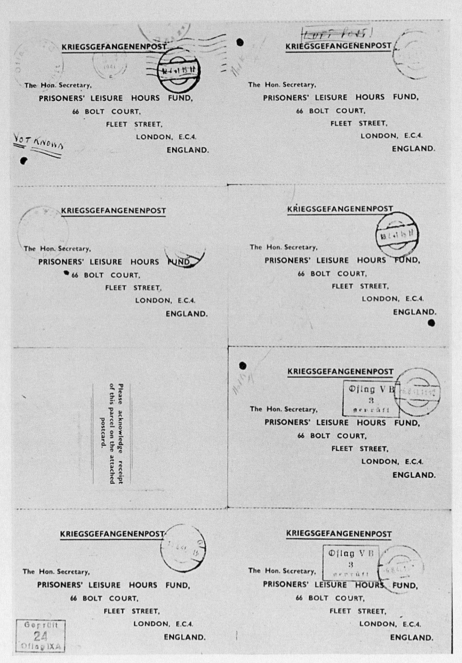

Note "Not Known" — and request on back of card.

D

ACKNOWLEDGEMENTS

To
The Hon. Secretary,
PRISONERS' LEISURE HOURS FUND,
66 BOLT COURT, FLEET STREET,
LONDON, E.C.4, ENGLAND.

Date: *July 23rd 1941*

Parcel No. *712*   Containing:

2 prs. socks
2 prs. pants (long)
2 vests
1 Jersey
1 pr. boots

has been received by me. *with very many thanks*
(Signed) *Hugh R. O'Sullivan Capt.*

To
The Hon. Secretary,
PRISONERS' LEISURE HOURS FUND,
66 BOLT COURT, FLEET STREET,
LONDON, E.C.4, ENGLAND.

Date: *5/7/41*

Parcel No. *715*   Containing:

2 prs. socks
2 prs. pants
1 vest
1 jersey
1 pr. boots

has been received by me. *with v. many thanks*
(Signed) *P.J. Maud   CAPT   P.J. MAUD   PoW No 1371*

To
The Hon. Secretary,
PRISONERS' LEISURE HOURS FUND,
66 BOLT COURT, FLEET STREET,
LONDON, E.C.4, ENGLAND.

Date: *31st July '41*

Parcel No. *714*   Containing:

2 prs. Sox
2 prs. Pants
2 Vests
1 Jersey
1 pr. Boots.

has been received by me.
(Signed) *A.J. Young*

To
The Hon. Secretary,
PRISONERS' LEISURE HOURS FUND,
66 BOLT COURT, FLEET STREET,
LONDON, E.C.4, ENGLAND.

Date: *30-7-41*

Parcel No. *716*   Containing:

2 prs. Sox
2 prs. Pants
2 Vests
Jersey
1 pr. Shoes.

has been received by me.
(Signed)

To
The Hon. Secretary,
PRISONERS' LEISURE HOURS FUND,
66 BOLT COURT, FLEET STREET,
LONDON, E.C.4, ENGLAND.

Date: *8 July '41*

Parcel No. *713*   Containing:

2 prs. socks
2 prs. pants
2 vests
1 Jersey
1 pr. Boots

has been received by me.
(Signed)

To
The Hon. Secretary,
PRISONERS' LEISURE HOURS FUND,
66 BOLT COURT, FLEET STREET,
LONDON, E.C.4, ENGLAND.

Date: *29th July '41*

Parcel No. *711*   Containing:
1 Suit case
2 prs. Socks
2 prs. Pants
2 Vests
1 jersey
1 pr. Boots
1 pr. laces

has been received by me.
(Signed)

To
The Hon. Secretary,
PRISONERS' LEISURE HOURS FUND,
66 BOLT COURT, FLEET STREET,
LONDON, E.C.4, ENGLAND.

Date: *August 11th*

Parcel No. *1*   Containing:

Shoes - (my size = 10)
Shirts & collars
underclothes
Socks

has been received by me. *with thanks*
(Signed) *J.F.H. Surtees*

PRISONERS' LEISURE HOURS FUND

Parcel No.   1263

Contents:—
   1 Pr. Boots or Shoes (size)
   1 Woollen Jersey
   4 Undergarments
   4 Shirts
   2 Prs. Sox

Addressed to:—
   2/Lt. J.F.H. Surtees

Camp   Stalag XXA

Checked by   *R.R.*
Date   11.6.41   (see over)

Note acknowledgements of clothes from P.L.H.F., thus giving proof that the Red Cross
was not the only Society "accepted" by the Germans.

ACKNOWLEDGEMENTS

KRIEGSGEFANGENENPOST

The Hon. Secretary,
PRISONERS' LEISURE HOURS FUND,
66 BOLT COURT,
FLEET STREET,
LONDON, E.C.4.
ENGLAND.

KRIEGSGEFANGENENPOST

The Hon. Secretary,
PRISONERS' LEISURE HOURS FUND,
66 BOLT COURT,
FLEET STREET,
LONDON, E.C.4.
ENGLAND.

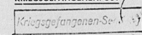

KRIEGSGEFANGENENPOST

The Hon. Secretary,
PRISONERS' LEISURE HOURS FUND,
66 BOLT COURT,
FLEET STREET,
LONDON, E.C.4.
ENGLAND.

KRIEGSGEFANGENENPOST

The Hon. Secretary,
PRISONERS' LEISURE HOURS FUND,
66 BOLT COURT,
FLEET STREET,
LONDON, E.C.4.
ENGLAND.

KRIEGSGEFANGENENPOST

The Hon. Secretary,
PRISONERS' LEISURE HOURS FUND,
66 BOLT COURT,
FLEET STREET,
LONDON, E.C.4.
ENGLAND.

Geprüft
24
Oflag IXA

KRIEGSGEFANGENENPOST

The Hon. Secretary,
PRISONERS' LEISURE HOURS FUND,
66 BOLT COURT,
FLEET STREET,
LONDON, E.C.4.
ENGLAND.

Geprüft
24
Oflag IXA

KRIEGSGEFANGENENPOST

The Hon. Secretary,
PRISONERS' LEISURE HOURS FUND,
66 BOLT COURT,
FLEET STREET,
LONDON, E.C.4.
ENGLAND.

KRIEGSGEFANGENENPOST

The Hon. Secretary,
PRISONERS' LEISURE HOURS FUND,
66 BOLT COURT,
FLEET STREET,
LONDON, E.C.4.
ENGLAND.

Note different post
marks of Camps.

F

ACKNOWLEDGEMENTS

•

To
The Hon. Secretary,
PRISONERS' LEISURE HOURS FUND,
66 BOLT COURT, FLEET STREET,
LONDON, E.C.4, ENGLAND.

Date *Aug - 19th 1941*

Parcel No. *12321*   Containing:

5 Records

With many Thanks

has been received by me.

(Signed) *J. Moore, Major*

To
The Hon. Secretary,
PRISONERS' LEISURE HOURS FUND,
66 BOLT COURT, FLEET STREET,
LONDON, E.C.4, ENGLAND.

Date *22 Aug 1941*

Parcel No. *12317*   Containing:

5 Records

has been received by me.

(Signed) *M. Elgood*

To
The Hon. Secretary,
PRISONERS' LEISURE HOURS FUND,
66 BOLT COURT, FLEET STREET,
LONDON, E.C.4, ENGLAND.

Date *29 Aug 41*

Parcel No. *12313*   Containing:

5 Records

Very Many Thanks

(F. V. CORFIELD. No 1259. OFLAG IXA/H)

has been received by me.

(Signed) *F. V. Corfield*

To
The Hon. Secretary,
PRISONERS' LEISURE HOURS FUND,
66 BOLT COURT, FLEET STREET,
LONDON, E.C.4, ENGLAND.

Date *6. 8. 41.*

Parcel No. *12310*   Containing:

5 Gramaphone Records

has been received by me. *R.A.F. No 33303 P.O. W No 91.*

(Signed) *J. C. Breese 1st Lt. D.F.C. R.A.F. Stalag Luft I Germany*

To
The Hon. Secretary,
PRISONERS' LEISURE HOURS FUND,
66 BOLT COURT, FLEET STREET,
LONDON, E.C.4, ENGLAND.

Date *12 AUG 41*

Parcel No. *12322*   Containing:

five records catalogues

has been received by me.

(Signed) *W. H. Broadbent*

To
The Hon. Secretary,
PRISONERS' LEISURE HOURS FUND,
66 BOLT COURT, FLEET STREET,
LONDON, E.C.4, ENGLAND.

Date *20th August '41*

Parcel No. *12320*   Containing:

5 Records.

has been received by me.

(Signed) *R. C. H. Pilcher Lt:*

To
The Hon. Secretary,
PRISONERS' LEISURE HOURS FUND,
66 BOLT COURT, FLEET STREET,
LONDON, E.C.4, ENGLAND.

Date *16 Aug 41*

Parcel No. *12312*   Containing:

5 Records

has been received by me.

(Signed) *Archabbotte Capt*

To
The Hon. Secretary,
PRISONERS' LEISURE HOURS FUND,
66 BOLT COURT, FLEET STREET,
LONDON, E.C.4, ENGLAND.

Date *19/VIII/41*

Parcel No. *12311*   Containing:

Bitter Sweet
2 Capriccio Italien
Balalaika
New Moon

has been received by me. *with thanks*

(Signed)

Acknowledgements of " Naughty " records, (one " Naughty " record with every four " Doves "). (Page 43.)

ACKNOWLEDGEMENTS

Acknowledgements to
" Private individuals "—
for parcels.

*(All names and addresses
were "manufactured"
by M.I.9.)*

H

ACKNOWLEDGEMENTS

●

Acknowledgements of "Naughty" games, etc.   (Note remarks!)

ACKNOWLEDGEMENTS

Acknowledgement of
" Naughty " books.

The _____ 1940

Many thanks for the parcel posted the _____
in _____. I received it in good - bad (underline the
right word) condition. Put a duplicate of the address into the packet.

Notice!

1. Don't send anything which is forbidden!
2. Don't send perishables!
3. Put only the duplicate of the address and contents, but no further
   communication into the packet!
4. Take only the best packing materials! Wrap the packet carefully!
5. The address must be complete and legible

The _____ 1940

Many thanks for the parcel posted the _____
in _____. I received it in good - bad (underline the
right word) condition. Put a duplicate of the address into the packet.

Notice!

1. Don't send anything which is forbidden!
2. Don't send perishables!
3. Put only the duplicate of the address and contents, but no further
   communication into the packet!
4. Take only the best packing materials! Wrap the packet carefully!
5. The address must be complete and legible

The _____ 1940

Many thanks for the parcel posted the _____
in _____. I received it in good - bad (underline the
right word) condition. Put a duplicate of the address into the packet.

Notice!

1. Don't send anything which is forbidden!
2. Don't send perishables!
3. Put only the duplicate of the address and contents, but no further
   communication into the packet!
4. Take only the best packing materials! Wrap the packet carefully!
5. The address must be complete and legible

The _____ 1940

Many thanks for the parcel posted the _____
in _____. I received it in good - bad (underline the
right word) condition. Put a duplicate of the address into the packet.

Notice!

1. Don't send anything which is forbidden!
2. Don't send perishables!
3. Put only the duplicate of the address and contents, but no further
   communication into the packet!
4. Take only the best packing materials! Wrap the packet carefully!
5. The address must be complete and legible

Datum _____

The _____ 1940

Many thanks for the parcel posted the _____
in _____. I received it in good - bad (underline the
right word) condition. Put a duplicate of the address into the packet.

Notice!

1. Don't send anything which is forbidden!
2. Don't send perishables!
3. Put only the duplicate of the address and contents, but no further
   communication into the packet!
4. Take only the best packing materials! Wrap the packet carefully!
5. The address must be complete and legible

The _____ 1941

Many thanks for the parcel posted the _____
in _____. I received it in good - bad (underline the
right word) condition. Put a duplicate of the address into the packet.

Notice!

1. Don't send anything which is forbidden!
2. Don't send perishables!
3. Put only the duplicate of the address and contents, but no further
   communication into the packet!
4. Take only the best packing materials! Wrap the packet carefully!
5. The address must be complete and legible

The 30 Aug 1941

Many thanks for the parcel posted the _____
in _____. I received it in good - bad (underline the
right word) condition. Put a duplicate of the address into the packet.

Notice!

1. Don't send anything which is forbidden!
2. Don't send perishables!
3. Put only the duplicate of the address and contents, but no further
   communication into the packet!
4. Take only the best packing materials! Wrap the packet carefully!
5. The address must be complete and legible

ACKNOWLEDGEMENTS

●

Acknowledgements of Games
and *Books*.

Note :
The Rev. C. O. Verrall, M.A.
(Cover all)
had his vicarage bombed by
the enemy ! He accordingly
sent all the remaining books
from his very old library !

I

ACKNOWLEDGEMENTS

●

M.I.9
" Phoney addresses. "
Acknowledgements.

●

62

ACKNOWLEDGEMENTS

Acknowledgements in *clear* of " Naughty " Goods.

ACKNOWLEDGEMENTS

●

COPY POSTCARD FROM CAPT. G.F.K. DALY, SULMONA
ITALY to THE HON. SECRETARY, PRISONERS'
LEISURE HOURS FUND, 66, BOLT COURT, FLEET
STREET, LONDON, E.C.4.

21/8/41.

Dear Secretary,

The words quoted at the
head of your notepaper by G. Runyan are
apt. Space is certainly rather limited.
No grounds for useless discouragement, in
fact! One is here a prisoner & so must
meet the inevitable boredom with one's
head high. The spiritual and material
necessities supplied by you with such
generosity make camp life very much easier
to cope with. Already the fourth clothing
parcel of the May lot has arrived. Some
six weeks slower than usual, all the same
they have got here. Quite safely, too, and
complete.

I want to thank you, but find difficulty
in expressing what it means to us to know we
have such kind friends thinking of us at
home. Major Pritchard, Lieut. Deane-Drummond
and 2nd. Lieut. Paterson join me in my most
sincere thanks for your very real kindness.

Yours Ever,

G.F.K. Daly.

Capt.

One of the many acknowledgements to M.I.9 indicating the activities
were well known — and appreciated.

MESSAGE

●

PRIME MINISTER'S
PERSONAL MINUTE

3A

10, Downing Street,
Whitehall.

SERIAL No   M 788 /.

Message from the Prime Minister
to the Prisoners of War.

In this great struggle in which we are engaged,
my thoughts are often with you who have had the misfortune
to fall into the hands of the Nazi.

Your lot is a hard one, but it will help you
to keep your courage up to know that all is well at home.
Never has the country been so completely united in its
determination to exterminate Nazidom and re-establish
freedom in the world.   Our strength grows daily, and
assistance flows from America in ever-increasing volume.
In high-hearted confidence we press forward steadily along
the road to certain victory.

Keep yourselves fit in mind and body, so that
you may the better serve our land, and, when peace comes,
play your part in establishing a happier, safer homeland.

God bless you all.

Winston Churchill

August 3, 1941.

One of the many "invisible" messages sent on cotton handkerchief.
(See Page 42.)

ESCAPE AIDS

SPECIAL WIRELESS RECEIVERS

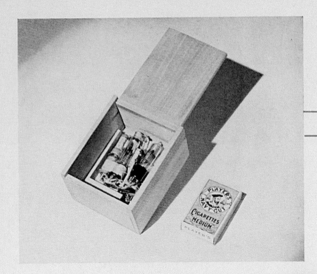

Cigar Box Type.   Range 400 miles.

6″ x 6″ x 1⅞″.   Range 700 miles.

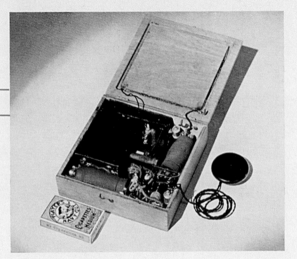

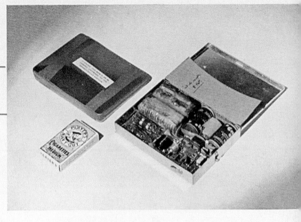

WIRELESS
TRANSMITTERS

Note Telescopic 2′ 6″ Mast.

100 Players Cigarette Tin Type.
Range 100 miles.

SPECIAL WIRELESS RECEIVERS.

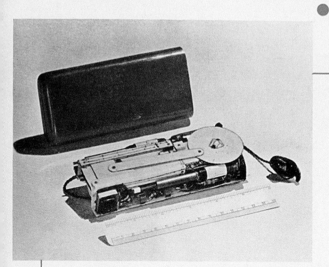

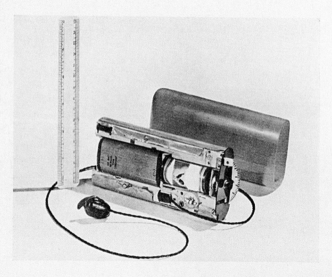

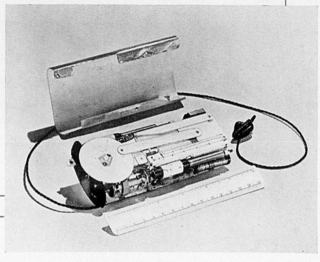

3 Cigar Case Size. Range 250 miles.

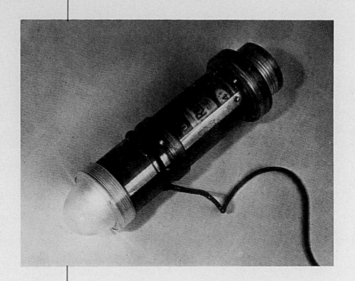

This Torch is constructed of acetate. It weighs 6 ozs. It is watertight.

It is bottom heavy. The user can either Morse if capable of doing so, or if overcome through fatigue or enemy action can, by turning bottom, keep torch alight for twenty-four hours. It is fitted with lanyard, and floats in water as shown in the lower illustration.

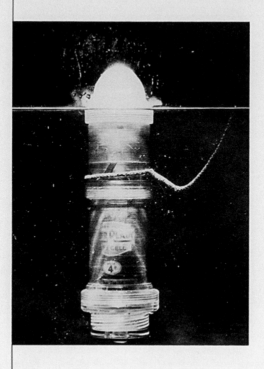

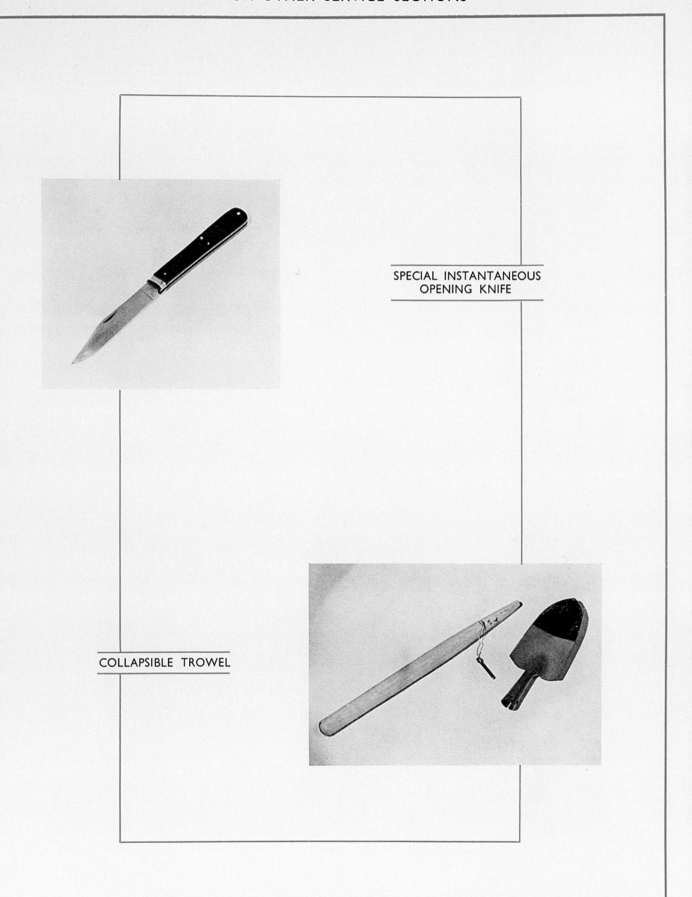

SPECIAL INSTANTANEOUS
OPENING KNIFE

COLLAPSIBLE TROWEL

GERMAN AIR FORCE
OFFICER.

OTHER RANKS.

GERMAN INFANTRY.

"TWO WAY" COAT

"Newmarket"

GERMAN STEEL HELMET

Exact in every detail.

●

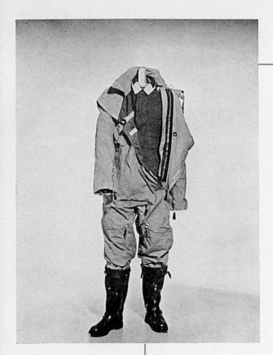

GERMAN
PARACHUTIST

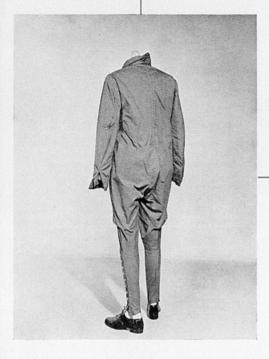

NORWEGIAN

SPANISH
TUNIC

Part of the functions of M.I.9 was to produce Foreign costumes — of all combatants.

These were produced in exact detail.

The copies could not be distinguished from the originals.

SPANISH
GREATCOAT

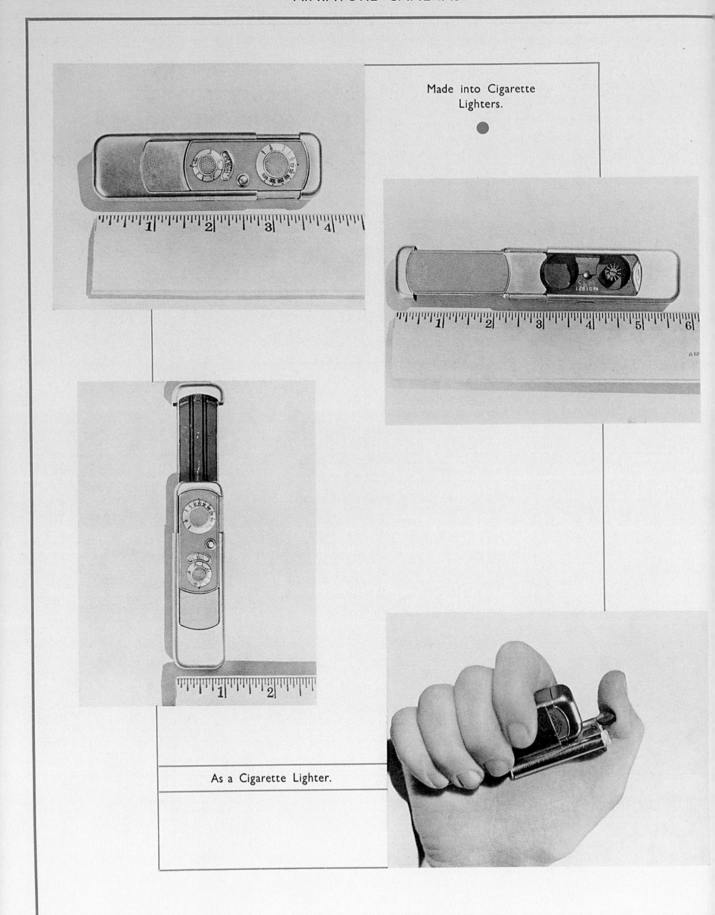

Made into Cigarette Lighters.

As a Cigarette Lighter.

PART THREE

SOURCES

© IWM unless otherwise stated

Research Notes for M R D Foot and J M Langley's 'MI9: Escape and Evasion, 1939–1945' (Documents.25378) © Rights Holder

Maps C.49.e.55, The British Library

AIR 1/1976/204/273/48, The National Archives

RAF Section: Exhibits II: 3 Exhibit Caption Enquiries (EN1/2/EXH/002/3)

RAF Section: Exhibits II: 4 Miscellaneous Exhibits (EN1/2/EXH/002/4)

Private Papers of Lieutenant L A Wingfield MC DFC (Documents.18776) © Rights Holder

Private Papers of Miss M K Howat (Documents.16229) © Rights Holder

TS 28/581, The National Archives Trophies – Air Force (EN2/1/TRO/002/1)

BOOKS BY M.I.9 LECTURERS

Bosanquet, David, *Escape Through China: Survival After the Fall of Hong Kong* (London: Robert Hale, 1983)

Cartwright, H A, and Harrison, M C C, *Within Four Walls* (London: Edward Arnold, 1930)

Durnford, Hugh George, *The Tunnellers of Holzminden* (Cambridge: Cambridge University Press,1920)

Hervey, H E, *Cage-Birds* (London: Penguin, 1940)

Keeling, Edward Herbert, *Adventures in Turkey and Russia* (London: John Murray, 1924)

McCormac, Charles, *'You'll Die in Singapore'* (London: Robert Hale, 1954)

Nabarro, Derrick, *Wait for the Dawn* (London: Cassell & Co, 1952)

PUBLICATIONS

Baldwin, R E, *Behind Enemy Lines: Evasion and Escape Aids of World War II* (Louisville: Frazier History Museum, 2013)

Froom, Phil, *Evasion & Escape Devices: Produced by MI9, MIS-X & SOE in World War II* (Pennsylvania: Schiffer Publishing Ltd, 2015)

Bond, Barbara, *Great Escapes: The Story of MI9's Second World War Escape and Evasion Maps* (London: Times Books, 2015)

Hutton, C Clayton, *Official Secret: The Remarkable Story of Escape Aids* (London: Max Parrish, 1960)

Hutton, Clayton, *The Hidden Catch* (London: Elek Books, 1955)

Evans, A J, *The Escaping Club* (London: The Bodley Head, 1921)

Evans, A J, *Heir to Adventure: Notes for an Autobiography* (London: Unifax, 1961)

Insall, A J, *Observer: Memoirs of the RFC, 1915–1918* (London: William Kimber, 1970)

IMAGE LIST

© IWM unless otherwise stated

Art.IWM ART 2629 © Rights Holder, ZZZ 7150D, HU 54527, Q 69484 © Rights Holder, EPH 810, EPH 809, Q 60299 © Rights Holder, Q 31452, X007-1069/002/004 © RAF Museum, EPH 4397 © Rights Holder

ACKNOWLEDGEMENTS

The author of the introduction would like to thank everyone at IWM who has been involved in the task of making this little-known volume more widely available. These include Publishing Officer Lara Bateman, Designer Kirsty Macdiarmid, Museum Archivist Sarah Henning, curatorial colleagues Alan Wakefield and Stephen Walton, Margaret Weller's Visual Resources team, Head of Collections Access and Research Maria Castrillo, Librarian Jane Rosen and the Research Room and Project Delivery teams. I hope that Leila Harris, Stephanie Balk and Tara Fitzgerald may find something in these pages to make them smile.

I am also indebted to many people outside IWM who I have discussed this subject with or who have provided help. These include Dr Will Butler, Dr Helen Fry, Dr Tony Insall, Juliette Johnstone, Fred Judge, Steven Kippax, Eric Mercer, Michael Paterson, Ian Piper, Lee Richards, Phil Tomaselli and Henry Weeds. Belinda Haley from the Royal Air Force Museum has provided invaluable assistance. I am also grateful to the staff of the British Library, Guildhall Library and The National Archives who have been very accommodating in providing access to research materials.

ABOUT THE CURATOR

Sarah Paterson is a Curator in the First World War team. She joined IWM as a librarian in 1988 and has worked in various different capacities including being the IWM family history lead. Her areas of particular interest include POW, women and conflict, military families and the British Occupation of Germany after both world wars.